The Art of Living Seasonally

Willa Daniels

Willa Daniels

The Art of Living Seasonally

Willa Daniels

The Art of Living Seasonally
Copyright © 2023 by Willa Daniels

First Edition: May 2023
This edition was first published in 2019

Cover design by Rebecacovers
Leaf divider image: Freepik.com
Tree image by OpenClipart-Vectors from Pixabay
Snowflake image by OpenClipart-Vectors from Pixabay
Candle image by Shahid Abdullah from Pixabay
Egg image by Hung Nguyen from Pixabay
Flower image by Jennifer R. from Pixabay
Sun image by OpenClipart-Vectors from Pixabay
Wheat image by OpenClipart-Vectors from Pixabay
Apple image by Kickie A from Pixabay
Fall leaf image by Monfocus from Pixabay
Holly image by aalmeidah from Pixabay

ISBN: 978-1-7377499-9-8 (Paperback)
ISBN: 978-1-7377499-8-1 (eBook)

Printed in the United States of America
Published by: Serenity Endeavors Press
jenflanaganbooks.com

Willa Daniels

Willa Daniels

Table of Contents

To my beautiful friends and family. You continue to encourage and inspire me.
Thank you all.

A special thanks to Christy, Kellie, Sarah, Jana, Brie, Sheila, and Dutch for beta reading.
Dutch for everything. Always.
Cait for always believing me.
My family and friends for their endless support.
This beautiful world and its infinite inspiration.

Triple love to above.

Willa Daniels

The Art of Living Seasonally

Foreword

Each year, the world around us moves through the seasons in a definitive cycle. Budding and growing anew every spring, it becomes stronger with every passing month before it's time to harvest and store up resources for the winter and the rejuvenation period.

There was a time when we, as people, followed a similar path. A time when we lived closer to the earth in a more symbiotic relationship. I believe there is a benefit to applying some of these practices. There is a calming simplicity and definite beauty to being aware of the passage of time. To embracing and even celebrating these changes as we appreciate each year and what it brings.

When we think about the fact that we will see only eighty or so springtimes, with all their floral beauty, it seems like such a small number. Approximately eighty times, we'll see the apple trees bud. It's not meant to be depressing, but rather to remind us that we are here for only a short time and we should appreciate everything we receive. For, our experiences and memories are all we get to take with us.

Even athletes have found the benefit of an annual cycle of training to achieve the best results. Allowing a break between training cycles encourages healing and further growth the following year.

Many calendars of our civilizations begin the year in the winter, and I feel it appropriate to do so as well, as this prepares us for the year to come. However, feel free to begin wherever you are currently in the cycle of the year.

Also, don't restrict yourself to a specific day. Depending on the region you live in, harvest can be early or late. The suggested dates I've listed are for the Northern Hemisphere, but if you live in the Southern Hemisphere, your seasons are inverted. Adjust accordingly. Do what feels right.

By splitting up the year into four seasons and then in mid-seasons, we interestingly align with many established holidays around the world. In each season and mid-season, we see different changes happening on the earth. They are outlined here to reflect upon. Looking for these changes throughout the year helps us connect with the natural cycle and strengthens our bond with time, age, and the world around us. Suggestions are also listed with ideas of fun things to do to celebrate and acknowledge the changing seasons.

Significant events are often marked with ceremonies, rituals, or traditions. Things like wedding ceremonies, annual fireworks, or holiday baking are common celebrations. Celebrating the passing of time or important occasions of our life with these traditions strengthens our bonds with time and with those who matter to us. Try adding some of these celebrations to your annual events to facilitate a more nature-focused year.

Traditionally, we would have eaten differently as the seasons progressed. For example, we would have eaten fresh fruit in the spring and summer, heavier foods during harvest, and hearty soups from stored foods over winter.

Some nutrition studies say the only common factor between the diets of the healthiest, longest-living people in the world is that they were prepared with human hands. I believe it's important for the majority of our food to be eaten as fresh as it can, as it retains more nutrients. And if our meals are prepared by human hands, with the purpose of providing healing and nourishment, it somehow passes on even more wellness. Any step towards eating a little closer to the earth is a win.

Just as the cycle of the earth has yearly improvements, I have included life-goal plans to achieve what you want out of your life. These can be as simple or as complex as you like. We all want different things from life, but if we don't plan for them, they're much less likely to materialize. Having a picture of where we want to go helps us get there, even if we don't have a large number of material goals.

To further this connection, I've included suggestions for goal planning according to the season. In the winter, you'll reflect and plan, while taking the time to rejuvenate. In the spring, you'll begin again, fresh and new, excited about the year ahead. In the summer, you'll be in the thick of it, getting things done but remembering to take some time to enjoy this beautiful life. In the fall, you'll get to celebrate all the accomplishments from the year so far and start prepping for the winter months, where you will be less active, to rest and restart this cycle.

I suggest getting a journal or notebook to use alongside this book. I personally enjoy the feel of a pencil making notes across the paper. Electronic documents are fine too, but you'll want something easy to take along with you.

This pattern of planning and action throughout the year, plus being aware of the changing seasons, helps us connect with nature and shift to a purer state of being. It also helps us realize our best self and not only acknowledge what we want out of life, but to finally achieve what we've always wanted.

It's within our grasp, beautifully, easily, and with the rhythm of the world around us that we often don't even notice.

How to Winter!

Overview
December 20-23 (Winter Solstice / Christmas / Yule)

Solstice translates to "the sun stands still." This is because, on this day, the sun appears to pause, stilled at the edge of the horizon, and reverse its path. This is also the longest night of the year, when the nighttime hours are at their peak. After this point, sunlight is won back every day, little by little, a sure promise of spring to come.

Wintertime is often seen as a dead cycle. It's the time of year when plants are dead and the trees are without leaves. Instead, think of winter as a cycle of rejuvenation. Yes, some plants die, but most of them, trees included, simply hibernate. They retract within themselves to withstand the cold temperatures. Storing their life force for a flourishing rebirth in the spring.

In a cyclical pattern aligned with the human aging process, converse to the rebirth we see in the spring, this would be the elders at the end of their lifetime. My favorite way to think about this isn't to feel as though we're weak or fragile but, instead, that we are full of wisdom and experience from the year!

What to Do

Focus your time on a little self-healing, soul-searching, and rejuvenation. Appreciate the wisdom you have gained this year and how that will aid you in the coming one. You are in a unique position to be objective when you can take the time to step back and assess your progress.

You have spent the previous year accomplishing many things, and this is the time to retrospect. What went well this year, and what didn't? What do you want to change for the coming one?

Make sure to employ some self-love and not judge yourself harshly when things don't go as well. We all learn throughout our lives. Instead of having the expectation that you should have known it before, take the lesson now, make observations, and adjust. Perfection is an illusion. Aim for progress instead.

Enjoy the season. Take time for yourself, in whatever manner you prefer. It may mean taking baths with a book or a candle, or catching up on your favorite shows. You may enjoy hiking or spending time rereading your favorite book.

It's not a coincidence that we associate smells like cinnamon, orange, and clove with this time of year. These herbs are well known for their ability to strengthen the immune system and allay illnesses. Enjoy baked goods with these flavors, or make pomanders to hang or set around the house. Pomanders are made by scoring an orange and studding it with cloves. Roll the pomanders in a mixture of powdered holiday spices until fully dry (two to three weeks). Try scoring the orange in fun patterns. The scent intensifies as it dries. Hang with a ribbon or thread with string and needle. They are also pretty, set in a bowl.

Try making ornaments with cinnamon, clove, and nutmeg. There are several recipes available. A good one is to mix 1 cup of spices, ½ cup of applesauce, and ½ cup of glue. Another favorite recipe only uses spices and applesauce. Mix some of each together until you get a dough thick enough to shape. Mix and roll between parchment papers until ¼ inch thick, then use cookie cutters to cut it into holiday shapes. A few drops of water will fix any cracks. Make sure to use a toothpick or straw to make a hole at the top for hanging. Bake at 200 for 2 hours, flipping them halfway through baking. Let them sit overnight to finish hardening. Decorate with paint, glitter, or stamps. Add a ribbon or yarn so you can hang them. They smell amazing while baking and hanging.

Of course, any baked goods can be made special when they involve friends or family. I fondly remember making Christmas holiday cookies with my parents and sister every year. It was an important enough event that we would mark it on the calendar so we could all be together. If you try this with little ones, one tip I'll add is to use jelly roll pans under the cookies while decorating. Little kids love adding sprinkles, and it goes everywhere! The pans help contain most of the fun.

Don't forget the purpose of the holiday season: spending time celebrating the culmination of the year with friends and family. Don't get so caught up in the overloaded to-dos that you lose sight of that. Challenge yourself to get rid of things on your to-do list. What's your priority? Can you mark some of it for a future year? The rest doesn't matter as much.

Gifts can be simple, homemade gestures of love. Or even better, they can be an outing. Invite your friend to lunch, a pottery class, a painting class, or to donate time together for community service.

Often, for me, this means beginning the day with a cup of coffee with no focus on the day until I get to work. My weekends allow more time for relaxation, maybe with a book, pushing off any small items I need to do until later in the day. After work, I try to sit for a while, planning my next day, before jumping into anything else, and I ensure I have several days with no agenda after work during the week. I try to spread out what little I have to do throughout the week or push it off until spring.

This is also a great time to catch up with old friends. I like to schedule a dinner with one or more of my friends 2-4 times a month, depending on other plans, so we can catch up and celebrate time together. We also typically have a big Holiday Open House, where people stop by whenever it works for them during a set time and we can all visit together.

Take more time to sleep. Before electricity, we would have slept more, relaxed more, and spent more time with friends and family. The lack of daytime meant time sitting around the fire or lamps to talk or play music. Our ancestors would have gone to bed earlier as well since oil and candles weren't cheap. Take the earth's advice. Fewer daytime hours should mean less active time.

In addition to holiday planning, schedule time for yourself in the upcoming months. Maybe dream about your next vacation. Winter has comfort in store for you. Enjoy the darker, colder months. Snuggle in warm, cozy socks in front of the fireplace. Aim for more time at home, more sleep, and more time to yourself.

Goals

Finally, I plan. I make tweaks to my big-picture dream, make a list of things to accomplish this coming year, create a goal plan, and write out steps for it.

Just like all large companies have a goal plan or strategic direction, we need one as well. If you don't have an end goal in mind, how do you know what paths to take throughout the year? The daily decisions we make often limit our following choices. Without a plan, we could inadvertently make decisions that would make getting what we want additionally difficult, if not impossible. Knowing your goals helps you make decisions to ensure your choices fit with your ultimate objective. As you plan, ask yourself how each activity fits in as a priority for this year's accomplishments.

1. *Big-Picture Dream:* To start your plan, it's important to first have a dream. Take some time in quiet introspection and create a dream for your future. Don't worry about any format. Think about what you would like your day to look like 10 years in the future.

    Describe your day. What takes up the hours of your day? What about your typical week?

    Write this out in whatever form feels natural. It could be a journal or a Word document. Just remember you will tweak this every year, as you are constantly changing. You will want it easy to find, take with you, and update.

    Make a pie chart, and think about the number of hours a day you would like to spend on different activities, such as work, time with family, friends, community service, exercising, relaxing, reading, etc. Think about what this pie chart would look like for today and compare the two. Are they similar? Why not? What adjustments would you like to make? Some may be immediate, while others will be a future goal.

    Rules: Dream big. Don't let your fears derail you at this stage. This is your chance to dream and do whatever your heart desires. Your ability to be creative and plan will expand beyond your normal, logical mind if you stick to the dream-like parameters here. When you work on the actual plan you seek to accomplish, you'll be making more analytical decisions. It doesn't belong here.

Do this activity in one sitting to fully embrace it. This is all you are accomplishing on this day.

2. *Annual Goals:* Make a separate list of things you want to accomplish in the coming year. Be specific. Be simple. These may be things you want to do around the house, craft projects, or decluttering. It could also be relationships you want to improve. I always have a few things I want to work on personally, such as being more present, being less judgmental, or to improve body-image issues.

Ideas to get you thinking: improve health, improve finances, connect with purpose, help others, travel, new habits, improve relationships, try something new, change your environment, or go for an adventure.

Goals will be either intentional or actionable. The above ideas are generally intentional goals. Actionable goals would be painting the study, making a garden, or getting in shape. Often, your intentional goals will create several actionable goals.

If you're finding you have more than you think you can do in one year, create a list for future years. Don't pin them to a physical year at this point; just say they are future items. You can prioritize them later.

Sometimes, intentional goals repeat each year because they are important to your overall growth.

This activity should be done as a standalone one. Don't push yourself into action at this point. Write and rewrite. Take your time. Involve your family if you want a family goal plan.

3. *Intentional-Goal Plan:* Every goal you want to achieve this year should have a plan. This will be detailing how you will accomplish your item. Be as descriptive as you want; just remember it may have to change when you get into the action itself. That's okay and perfectly normal.

Each intentional goal is a separate activity. This allows us to fully think through the issues we are facing, where we want to be, and how we think we can get there. For example, if you're trying to be less judgmental, what's the cause of your judgmental behavior? Why do you immediately go there? What are some ideas to do things differently? What would it look like if you weren't judgmental? How would that feel? Really play with the thought, feel it out, and challenge it.

Intentional goals won't have a lot of action items. If they do, add them to your actionable goals. It could be things such as reading a book by Brené Brown to improve your leadership or knitting a special hat for a friend to improve show more love to your friends. Otherwise, intentional goals are for self-reflection. We will come back and check in with these throughout the year.

Do not let this activity cause stress. Sit down with your journal or laptop in a quiet spot, with a cup of hot tea or a glass of wine. Let yourself think about it a bit before writing. Then, let it go.

Take time to work through these. You don't have to do them all at once. Maybe break them up over a week or two.

4. *Actionable-Goal Plan:* We'll save this for the second half of winter. Focus on the self-reflection of the intentional-goal plan and on taking time for yourself.

In Summary

Although this night marks the longest night of the year, after this point, the days slowly stretch back to include more sunlight each day. Even in the darkest day, there's the promise of light. And remember, darkness doesn't always mean negativity or fear, but it can be a calm and retrospective moment for healing.

Remember to take time for yourself. Don't focus so much on the plan itself that you feel overwhelmed. It's for reflection, healing, and planning. Maybe you need to physically schedule "dates" with yourself to read, take a bath, or go to the coffee shop for a quiet time. It's critical to self-heal this time of year. Your body and mind need it.

Reflect on what you want to get out of the upcoming year. Build your most beautiful big-picture dream, and outline your annual goals. Take personal, introspective time to work through your intentional-goal plans. Use the wisdom of previous years to guide you on your path.

"It is the longest night.
The dark is battled by light.
Time for plans and reflection,
Friends and family affection,
And holiday celebrations delight!"

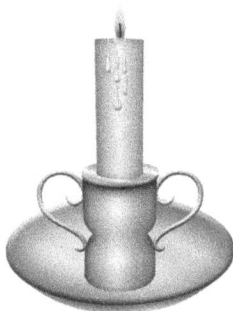

Mid-Winter

Overview

February 2nd (Groundhog Day / Candlemas)

Groundhog Day marks the first stirrings of spring. While it's still not fully here, the earth is slowly moving toward birth and renewal, with the sun being halfway between the winter solstice and the spring equinox.

In the United States, if our resident groundhog, Punxsutawney Phil, sees his shadow on this day, we get the full six more weeks of winter. If he doesn't see his shadow, spring will arrive early. The legend was originally of a badger or bear, depending on the country of origin. One story says that if the badger sunbathes the week of Candlemas, he'll be back in his hole for four more weeks. Either way, a mid-winter respite of cold indicates a longer winter.

Depending on where you live, you may see a few bulb shoots, like crocus, or new buds of leaves on trees. The weather may sporadically have warmer days, allowing us some time in the much-missed sun.

Regarding the light, not only can we liken it to the illumination of nature stirring to life, but also to ourselves. We are brightening and shining with the inspiration of the year ahead.

What to Do

Focus on the signs of nature around you in this time of purification from winter. When you notice sprouts forming, recognize the germination of seeds happening under the ground. Occasional rains and warmer weather are beginning to cleanse the earth. We also prepare to stretch and get back into the business of our year and goals ahead.

I also like to use this time of year to purge. It's cold outside and not always hospitable to spend much time there, so inside jobs feel good. I like to go through my closets and junk drawers, pulling out things I no longer use. Extra belongings take time to maintain, clean, and organize that could be spent on other endeavors. It's easier to find the things you want when there's less to rummage around. It also feels nice to open a closet to find that only the things you physically use are being stored within. Watch a YouTube video on minimalism or zero-waste living for inspiration. You don't have to take all their advice to find a few great ideas.

Celebrate the additional light. One older tradition was to light fires and candles in all the rooms just as the sun set to extend the light hours, even a few minutes longer, and to celebrate the return of the light and warmth. A fun way to carry on this tradition would be to turn on every light in your house or to light candles in each room, even for a few minutes, to participate and think about the changing seasons.

Spend time thinking about your inspirations, shining in this time for rejuvenation and rebirth. Imagine your creativity flowing with renewed energy. This is also the time to rededicate yourself to healthy practices and goals or to start new ones!

With the harvest being completed in the fall, historically, people would eat their stored food all winter. This is a great time to eat hearty meals with meats, root vegetables, and dried beans/peas.

Should you store any dried herbs from the season, use these liberally, as they provide necessary vitamins at a time typically without fresh vegetables. Season with dried spices (think chili or Indian food), as they are good for the immune system as well.

Goals

Brush off that goal plan we created weeks ago. See where you left off and what's left to finish. Make tweaks as necessary, but try not to radically rewrite it. You spent time and energy coming up with it. It's probably mostly complete. However, acknowledge that priorities and thoughts shift over time. Change is normal and healthy. This is your final preparation before the big work of the year. Feel free to start working on some of your goals if they are quick wins or coincide with this renewal phase. Good ideas would be a deep cleaning or a creative activity.

1. *Big-Picture Dream:* Read back over and make tweaks as necessary. Does it feel right? Is it still the place you want to be? Can you see yourself there? Spend some time *living* in this future vision of yourself. You can get there, but you need a solid picture on which to dream.

    Don't forget to dream big and not let logic and doubt restrict your picture.

2. *Annual Goals:* Review and tweak your goals for the year. Prioritize and calendar your actionable goals. Make a note next to them in which month or weeks you plan to do them. Spread them out throughout the year so you can physically accomplish them. Do this how ever works best for you.

    Take note of the times of year when you're typically busier than others with vacations or holidays. I typically load the beginning and middle of my year with goals, leaving wiggle room at the end of the year for unforeseen things and because I tend to be busier with the holidays and end-of-year preparations.

Transfer these actionable goal dates onto your house calendar or agenda planner. You can even add reminders to your phone or calendar apps. This holds you accountable for the goal, but it also helps you plan around the activity. For example, if I want to clean out my attic, I'll schedule that for spring, when it's not too hot or cold. It aligns with the spring cleaning feeling we tend to get, which inspires me to do the work. I can see it coming up on the calendar weeks earlier and mentally prepare myself for that weekend.

2. *Affirmations:* Affirmations are just declarations, things you say out loud to make a statement and affirm within yourself. Speaking the words out loud helps cement them into your mind and soul. The act keeps it fresh in your mind all day. Summarize your intentional goals into items so they are easy to reference daily or weekly.

Actionable goals, like "organize the attic," aren't needed here, as you'll set aside time during the year to accomplish these. However, you may be able to bucket some of the more actionable goals into a larger goal that may be helpful. "Unclutter/simplify my life" can be changed to "I live simply and do not need many things," or the goal "Be kind to myself and others" fits perfectly on its own.

Bucketing them isn't always right, though. Sometimes my affirmations combine several intentions, but alternatively, sometimes I'll have multiple affirmations for one intention. As with everything else, do what feels right.

Reword these summarized goals as though they will happen, positively and effortlessly. For example, "My life and mind will be less cluttered." Take a deep breath. See it, and feel how it will be when it's fully realized. Trust yourself.

Sometimes your affirmation doesn't look much like your goal. That's okay. Sometimes the positive affirmation needs to be worded differently to get you to your goal. It needs to be meaningful to actualize your goal. For example, the goal of "Reduce spending" could work with the affirmation "I live simply and do not need many things to be happy." Take your time with it.

Feel free to add extra affirmations as needed. Just keep it short enough so you can easily reflect on it. You may find you have similar goals from year to year and affirmations that cover several goals. The difference may just be in the action plan for that particular year.

I like to look back over my affirmations at least weekly to keep my mind on my goals. Write your short list of them, and put it in your wallet, on your dresser, inside your bathroom mirror, or in your agenda calendar for quick reference. Whatever works for you to frequently review and think about them.

An amazing routine would be to look over them in the mornings or evenings before bed. I especially like affirmations before bed. I can add a daily intention for the next day this way, especially if I have something specific to accomplish.

I am always amazed by the results when I use, "Tomorrow morning, I will wake refreshed and ready to start the day." I think about how it would feel to have an amazing morning and what that would look like. Have a hard meeting the next day? Try "I will be calm and relaxed in tomorrow's meeting. It will go exactly as planned. I will know the right words to say."

I like to add something heartfelt at the beginning or end of them, such as, "To achieve my goals," or "For my best self," or "In a healthy and positive manner."

Most importantly, envision it happening and how it feels when it happens. What does success mean for you? What would it look like or feel like? Feel it. Believe it. Manifest your goals!

Reminder: Affirmations work great for intention setting and helping you achieve your goals, but don't forget to put the work in as well. If you have a hard meeting the following day, you should still plan time to think through the meeting and your target audience. Consider the facts and the people in the room. What are their motivations? What are acceptable outcomes? Then, when you set your intentions the night before, you'll know you did your part, and it'll be even easier to visualize the meeting going well.

3. *Actionable-Goal Plans:* It's time to create a plan for your actionable goals. Just like with the intentional goals, each action item is a separate activity. However, depending on how it's going, you can do more than one goal each day. I like to work on them a couple of times a week and get through a few at a time.

   Some seem easy, like "Paint the study"; however, your action plan will include what supplies you need to purchase or what helpers you need to enlist to do things like moving the furniture. The point is to walk through the activity in such a way that it feels like you've already done it. This way, you've removed barriers like fear and hesitancy that cause procrastination. You'll also think of things you need to do to prep for your activity, things that often leave us frustrated or delays our projects. I've gotten ready to paint a room and realized I didn't have any paint rollers.

Again, don't do these all at once. You may find underlying issues arising from creating an actionable plan. There may be reasons why you haven't accomplished an item before now. This is a good time to think through those issues and how you want to go about achieving your goal. Journal it. Let yourself feel around the problems in the tasks. Be realistic; be kind to yourself.

Update your action plans to coordinate with the dates set in your goal plans. If I have prep work to do ahead of time, I'll add it to my calendar as well. Schedule a shopping trip to get tarps and paint rollers, call a friend to ask for help, or find an available truck to take items to donate weeks or months ahead of time.

In Summary
During this time of renewal and purification, notice the stirring of life in the earth. When you see nature cleansing itself or blossoming with life, equate that to what's going on in your life in relation to it. Be grateful for the additional light and warmth. Notice how this reflects in yourself as inspiration and creativity for the new year blossoming. Take time for yourself to realize your goals. See them happen. Feel them happen. Make them happen.

Go over your big-picture dream and annual goals, adding priorities and dates to the calendar. Create some meaningful affirmations to keep your intentions in mind daily or weekly. Finally, create actionable-goal plans to ensure you are ready to do the work, adding these to the calendar as well.

How to Spring!

Overview
March 20-23 (Spring Equinox)

Today is about balance. It's one of the two days a year when the daylight hours equal the nighttime ones. Old traditions celebrate the sun as the days grow longer. An old story says that when the sun rises on the first day of spring, it gives three great leaps of joy as it finally tips the balance against the night hours.

This time of year is also about rebirth and renewal, even more than mid-winter, as we can readily see physical signs of spring all around us. Not only do we see fresh buds on the trees and shoots from flower bulbs, but this is also the time of year livestock is born.

April, from the Latin verb "aperire," means "to open." While the spring equinox happens in March, the date is close enough to April to understand the reason for its naming. Our ancestors named the fourth month of the year to mark the earth's opening, or awakening, with spring.

Most of us are familiar with the phrase, "April showers bring May flowers." This is nature's spring cleaning. The rain cleanses and clears the land of the waste that accumulated over the stagnant winter. Today, it also cleans our roads and buildings of salt and grime. Notice how fresh the earth looks after it rains. Watch how the plants respond.

The egg has long been a symbol of spring as it symbolizes both the sun and rebirth. Old traditions exist to plant an egg in your garden as a symbol of new growth. Rabbits have been recognized for their well-known high fertility, even though, today, we see them paid tribute to both through molded chocolates and candies.

One European tradition molds butter into the shape of a lamb. When we think back on all these reminders of growth and rebirth, it's no wonder we equate eggs, rabbits, baby chicks, lambs, and bulb flowers, like daffodils, with this time of year. It's not just about sweets; as fun as they are to celebrate spring, they have a much deeper root in our history.

What to Do
One of my favorite things to do in the spring is to resume my walks. While I may not get outside every day, I aim for every other day, with some wiggle room for life. While I'm out, I look for shifts in the season. Search for plants starting to bloom. Gray skies are replaced with a shining sun. See how bright it is. Feel the warmth of it on your face. Soak up a little sun even if you still need to wear a coat. New smells emerge from the thawing ground and the ice melting, depending on where you live. Pay attention to what changes you see around you.

Do you hear the birds in the morning? Robins are historically one of the first signs of spring and lovely to see hopping around the yard. Insects, like bees, start to reappear, getting ready to visit flowers and gather pollen.

The fuzzy little buds on the trees are my favorite sign of spring, reminding me of baby-animal fur. Moss starts growing on things as the weather gets warmer and the ground dewy. The smell of moist earth always reminds me of spring. I like to get down and scrape away some of the old season's dead stems to look for my lavender's fresh, green stalks. However, be careful to leave some old growth until the freezing weather has fully passed. This provides shelter and insulation to those baby leaves.

Be patient with the weather. Too often, I hear people complain about the varying cold versus warm temperatures or a heavily rainy day. Try to be patient with Mother Nature after she slept all winter long. She will take a little time to fully wake and bring life back from below to above the earth. I like to think of it like she's flexing her muscles, getting ready for the season. It's a time of balance, remember?

And rain is necessary for fully cleansing and prepping for the new year. Like a good long shower in the morning to help us wake up and feel refreshed, but the earth is large and takes a bit more work to get everything clean.

Keeping with the renewal and rebirth theme, reaffirm your spark of life, and take action. Shake off your winter cloak and spring forward with confidence in your goal plans. It's a great time to start indoor seeds for your garden. Consider creating an outdoor space for reflection. I find it energizing to get outdoors and clean out the garden beds in preparation for the planting season.

I'm always amazed to see how much rubbish and trash has accumulated on the side of the road after the snow melts. Part of this is from the winter winds that blow debris around, but it's also from neglect and the desire to be outdoors less during the colder months. While it's always great to get out and pick up the trash you see, working to improve your yard or neighborhood goes a long way. Cleaning back brush and old growth assists the plants in their re-emergence from winter hibernation.

We like to color eggs in shades that remind us of spring. Some cultures hide them outside for a hunt, which is a great excuse to get out in the sun. We also like to make deviled eggs, egg salad, and scotch eggs. It's fun to play with the theme. There are fresh shoots of vegetables like asparagus, sprouts, peas, and young greens as well. These vegetables make a great spring salad or spring pasta with fresh cheese. Enjoy a seasonal feast to herald the season.

While you clean out some of the brush and twigs from your yard or garden, twist some of the flexible pieces into little nests for your colorful eggs; they will look very festive in them.

A fun thing to do with your kids would be to go out early on the first day of spring and jump three times in celebration of the light! And if a little dancing and wiggling ensue, all the better for it.

During this time of finding balance and renewal, what would you like to let go of? What new habits would you like to start? Plant seeds literally and figuratively. If these items aren't part of your goals for the year, consider adding them. Any plants you want to start from seed should be started now, but indoors in a place with daylight. You will want to be past the fear of frost before they move outdoors.

Think further on the theme of balance. In what areas is balance important? Male and female balance has many advantages in the world. There is also a balance between light and dark. Without the dark, we wouldn't appreciate the light. Without death, we couldn't have rebirth. Sometimes, this means the death of bad habits or relationships and the rebirth onto new enriching paths.

Goals
Hopefully, your goal plans are set from winter. If not, take some time to finish up any action plans or intentional-goal plans. This is where we *spring into action* on our goals for the year. Less time is spent on the planning process. Part of this

time is also used to check in on your progress. This holds you accountable and keeps your goals at the forefront of your mind.

1. *Big-Picture Dream:* Think about your dream. This is your inspiration. All the steps you take this year are to get you to this beautiful place. Take time to enjoy this thought. Soak in it. You've laid the foundation to achieve it and are ready to do the work. Don't forget to keep the dream alive and maintain distance from fear and doubt. Logic has no place in your dreams. It's useful, but not here.

2. *Annual Goals:* Unless you're adding something, you don't have to review these. Sometimes, I do, just to keep them fresh in my mind and make sure I didn't schedule any conflicting vacations or dinner plans.

3. *Affirmations:* Check in with your affirmations. Are you reviewing these with any frequency? Don't judge yourself if you haven't; that doesn't help. Consider adding a weekly reminder to your calendar to review them.

4. *Intentional-Goal Plans:* Even though your affirmations sum up your goals, read through everything you wrote once while thinking through your intentional goals. I find reviewing these plans every six weeks very beneficial. These plans are changes we want to see in our lives, so reviewing them reminds us of what we want to do, why, and how.

   As other thoughts come up, feel free to journal further or tweak your affirmations as needed.

5. *Actionable-Goal Plans:* Review these plans to make sure you are ready to work on the items you scheduled for the next two months.

Add any details you need to accomplish your upcoming goals. If you feel any hesitancy to jump into action, spend some time thinking through it to find out what's holding you back. It could be fear that you aren't capable or prepared enough.

Enlist a friend to talk it out, or ask for advice. It's normal to have some fear toward a job you've never done before. Chances are, you can find a friend who has experience and wouldn't mind giving you some pointers or even assisting you in your work.

If you need a confidence booster, close your eyes and see the goal in completion. What will it look like? What will it feel like to have it done? How will you feel once you've accomplished it? Hold onto that joy and satisfaction.

Whatever it takes, work to ensure all blockages are removed and all preparations have been made. You've got this.

In Summary
Spring is finally here! It's time to start fresh. Enjoy the sun, the warmth, and being outdoors more often. Notice the changes around you when you're outside or driving. Think about renewal and your fresh start for the year. Find your balance and think positively to the year ahead.

Spring marks the balance of day and night, light and darkness. Depending on where you live, you will see stirrings of spring at different times this season. The earth is finding its balance between the seasons as well. Be patient as it adjusts to the change from cold to warm.

Ready, set, go! Set your plan into action! You've planned and planned, thought through, and prepared. It's now time to get moving. Get out there, and do what's needed to accomplish your dreams.

> *"Farewell to wintry spirits and friends;*
> *On morrow we greet the spirits of Spring.*
> *Our blessings to thee as your way you wend;*
> *And merry we'll meet next winter again."*
> -Traditional Celtic Blessing

Mid-Spring

Overview
May 1 (May Day / Beltane)

Flowers are the name of the game this mid-season. Those green shoots of life we saw in early spring have bloomed, and we start enjoying the beautiful flowers around us. The forests are alive with new life. Fruit trees have flowers, germinating for summer fruits. Birds are gathering dead shrubs and twigs to make nests and lay eggs.

In old Germany, unmarried young men would cut down a fir tree and remove its branches on May Eve (April 30th). They would stand guard over it all night long. In the morning, they would hold their Maypole dance. Ribbons attached to the top would be held by the revelers dancing around the pole after dawn. Intertwining in and out, they created a colorful weave. At the end of the day's festivities, they burned the pole in a big bonfire.

Other cultures decorate a flowering tree or bush in their yard. Neighbors compete for the best decoration. It makes me think

of Clark Griswold with his holiday light competition. In old
Ireland, they celebrated Beltane as the beginning of summer.
This marks the day they drove their livestock to their summer
pastures.

In many cultures, a bonfire was present. They drove their cattle
through the smoke. People would jump through it, as well, for
good luck. It was a day of celebration, dancing around the
bonfire, and reuniting with others to celebrate the changing
seasons. Each person took a portion of the bonfire home at the
end of the night. The smoke was used to clean and clear their
house as well. Some would even use a bit of ash from the fire
to fertilize their gardens. It raises the pH and lowers the acid.
Note: This is not good for acid-loving plants such as berries,
azaleas, fruit trees, and potatoes.

The smoke from woods like cedar and fir, which were
commonly used, is also a natural insect repellent. Even the
Native Americans drove their cattle through wood and brush
smoke to rid them of pests and illness, which was helpful
during this cleansing and clearing time of year.

What to Do
There's color all around. Even if you don't have a lot of flowers
in your yard, you will likely notice all the fresh greenery
everywhere. What colors are in your yard? I'm always amazed
by all the many shades of green, especially after a long winter.
On your drive to work, in the morning, notice the flowering
trees and plants. See how many colors you can spot.

I like to notice the growth that occurs every day. After they
start emerging, my hostas sometimes grow 3-4 inches in one
day! I notice my neighbors' peonies and their steady growth.
The trees on my morning drive are particularly green in the
summer. I enjoy watching them each season. It makes me
happy to connect with them and see their changes, just as you
would enjoy the neighborhood kids' growth.

See how many shades of green you can observe. With all the rain still cleansing the earth and encouraging development, I find some beautiful little fuzzy moss growing on my tree trunks. I love the shades of green tinting the trunk. It contrasts so beautifully with the reddish colors of the maple leaves and the bright blue sky. There's so much color this time of year!

Notice birds' nests full of eggs or baby birds. Listen for the chirping in the morning. I miss this during winter and enjoy its return. I have a few songbird feeders scattered around the yard to draw them in, and I bring out my hummingbird feeders, stored indoors to prevent freezing.

Enjoy fresh berries. Strawberries are the perfect spring addition to a spinach-and-walnut salad with some fresh goat cheese. Or add raspberries and cream cheese on waffles, pancakes, or French toast. Drizzle some farm-fresh honey on fresh-baked goods or enjoy a honey cake to celebrate the season. With all the baby lambs, cows, and goats, cheese is certainly in season as well. And, oh, how I love a good cheese plate with fruit!

Edible flowers! I've even seen people make cookies and cakes with fresh, edible flowers. How pretty are violets, chamomile, or calendula flowers on simple powdered-sugar icing cookies! They adhere nicely and have a shiny look to top a sugar cookie or honey cake.

When I was young, we used to make May Day baskets full of flowers from our neighborhood, deliver them to our neighbors' porches, ring the bell, and run. Consider making a May basket, filling it with fresh-cut flowers and goodwill for someone in need of healing or company. Get your children involved if you can.

Help the kids make flower-chain crowns, bracelets, or necklaces. They can be simple or elaborate and can adorn your kitchen table for the evening dinner. Decorate your favorite bush or tree with ribbons or strung shells. Write wishes on the ribbons to make a wishing tree. Build a small fairy garden in a section of your flower or vegetable garden or in a special place in your yard.

Try making a Maypole! You can always build a smaller version. Use dowel rods with brightly colored ribbons either hot glued to the top or pinned with a pushpin. They can decorate your flower beds or vegetable gardens. You can weave them around the pole or let the ribbons flow freely. If left free, they can be used to scare away unwanted birds. You can make a smaller version with chopsticks and hot glue and use it as a hair stick to adorn a messy bun.

Clean out some of the brush and twigs from your flower and vegetable gardens. Trim your bushes and trees before they begin too much of the new growth cycle. Be sure to leave a little of the dead growth in the yard for birds' nests. I get a lot of joy from being back outside in the newly warmer weather. It feels good to prepare the yard for the coming season.

Some places have a citywide cleanup around Earth Day or Arbor Day, which is at the end of April. See if you can participate in the local trash pickup, animal habitat conservation, or recycling efforts. As we require oxygen to live, we literally need plants for survival. Any small action you can do to improve the natural ecosystem of your community helps.

Visit a local farm for fresh berries, honey, or lavender. Farmers markets are reopening with fresh fruit, vegetables, and flowers. If possible, support these local people who work hard to continue to bring local produce and life to your community.

If you're in an area that allows open burning, have a small bonfire yourself. Make sure to pay attention to local laws and fire safety. I'm not encouraging jumping over it, but enjoying a little bonfire at the end of a day spent working in the yard is something I especially enjoy. The evening will have cooler temps on these spring days. We often bring out blankets to wrap up in and either hot chocolate, coffee, or a glass of wine.

Grill or cook hot dogs and bratwurst on a stick over the bonfire. My kids love to make foil-wrapped packs of meat, veggies, and potatoes to tuck in near the coals. They customize their own foil packs and eat right out of them after they are done cooking. Be careful to cook any meat thoroughly. Always be alert around a fire and let adults manage the foil packs. They can steam when opening. Of course, s'mores are always sticky, great fun, regardless of age.

Open your windows, and let in some fresh air. This helps clean out germs and the stagnant air from winter. If you smudge, feel free to run it through your house to clear the air and pests. It's a good time for a deep clean. They call it spring cleaning for a reason! Wipe down counters, shake out rugs, and dust the corners.

I like doing yoga in my backyard when the weather gets nice. Try setting up a meditation or prayer spot outside. If you don't have a garden, consider looking for community garden programs in your area that you can get involved with.

Make a sleep or drawer sachet with fresh flowers from your yard. You can even add some essential oils to brighten the scent. Or simply bring in some flowers to decorate the house.

Plan your garden if you have one. If you started any seeds at the beginning of spring, it's now the time to bring them outside to put in the earth. It's a creative time of year, so try something new. Write a song, sing, draw, paint, or write. Create any kind of art, make any kind of music. Challenge yourself to do something new. Give birth to new things!

Goals

We're well into our goal plans at this point. Check in with them to make sure you're on track.

1. *Big-Picture Dream:* As with each season, I read back over my dream for inspiration. However, this is a good time to edit or update your dream. Maybe it's because of the rebirth in creativity and action, but I always have new thoughts to add here at this time.

2. *Annual Goals:* Review if you want to add anything.

3. *Affirmations:* Check in with your affirmations. Are you doing them? Do you find them helpful when you do?

4. *Intentional-Goal Plans:* Review your goals. Make sure you're working towards them, keeping these objectives alive. Feel free to update or add notes as needed.

    Sometimes, I start my mornings with a bullet journal, just to see how I'm feeling on a few important topics and to help keep them forefront in my mind. How are my relationships going, for instance? How am I feeling physically? This gives me a few dedicated seconds to think on each topic and make a short note. It can be as simple as a check mark for good or an arrow for needing to work on this area. Other times, I like journaling a few thoughts on the matter. It changes daily. Journals should work for the process, not the other way around.

5. *Actionable-Goal Plans:* Read back through your plans. Update your calendar with the next two months' activities. Ensure you don't have any conflicts. Get your mind wrapped around what you plan on doing in the coming weeks.

Are you on track, or are you adjusting your next six weeks to accommodate some of the items from the prior six weeks? If so, consider the reason. Maybe you need to find help. It's possible you need to adjust your expectations and set more realistic goals.

If you need to push off a few items to next year, do so. Don't schedule your time so full that you don't leave room to enjoy life. Spend some time with friends or family outside, noticing the sights and scents around you.

In Summary
Connect with the earth in a way that recognizes the change through the season. Appreciate it. Notice it. Smell the damp earth and the blooming flowers. Open your windows to bring in fresh air. Bring in the fragrant, colorful blossoms. Enjoy the bright colors in nature.

Breathe your own new life by planting or creating something. Relish in the prepping for the abundance in the year to come. Committing to your plans will help you maintain an optimistic outlook for the future, continued growth, and prosperity. Celebrate the work you've done to set the stage for a great year and any activities already completed.

It's a time for courage, passion, and self-expression. Use this to your advantage as you celebrate the season with the changes within and without. Embrace the days ahead.

"The sullen winter nearly spent,
Queen Flora to her garden went.
To call the flowers from their sleep,
The years glad festivities to keep."
-Flora's feast: a masque of flowers. (London Cassell 1889) Crane, Walter
(1845-1915)

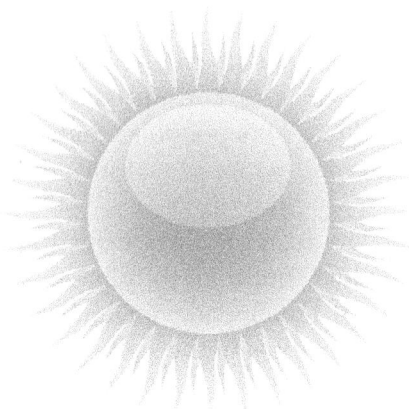

How to Summer!

Overview
June 21-23 (Summer Solstice)

The sun reaches its zenith today, with fifteen full hours of sun, marking it as the longest day of the year. It's time to celebrate the warm summer sun and the successes from spring's planting, both literally and figuratively. The planting is done, and life gets a little easier as we tend to what we've planted. It's time to pause for a celebration before the work of the harvest.

From the winter solstice to this day, the sun has been moving closer to the earth. It has been heating the soil. Flowers, fruits, and plants have been blooming, fragrant and full of life. After today, the days shorten, and the plants finish their cycle of growth and begin to slowly die until the winter solstice. So, today we celebrate the sun's fiery energy at its peak and bask in the light and abundance.

In England, rural villagers built a big bonfire on Midsummer's Night, called "setting the watch," to keep evil spirits away. If you jumped over it, you would have good luck for the coming year. Being blackened by the fire was considered very fortuitous. After the flames had burned and the ashes gone cold, they were used to protect their livestock or were scattered in their gardens for bountiful crops. The Celts celebrated Alban Hefin to honor the solstice with a bonfire under the skies. Pebbles would be carried around the bonfire and tossed into the flames with a wish or a prayer.

Sunwheels were used across Europe to celebrate the solstice. The wheel or a large ball of straw was lit on fire and rolled down a hill into a river. The burned remnants were taken into town and put on display. The people of Wales believed if the fire went out before the wheel hit the water, a good crop was guaranteed. Norse celebrations set a wagon wheel on fire, either incorporated into their bonfire or set rolling down a hill as they chased after it.

Legend has it, if you stay up at night, sitting in the middle of a stone circle on the summer solstice, you will see faeries. Be careful, though, because you can get lost by being led astray by the tricksters. Safeguard yourself by turning your clothing or jacket inside out to confuse them or by carrying a few leaves of rue in your pocket!

What to Do
Spend as much time outside as possible, soaking up the sun's rays! If you can get out at lunchtime to see the sun at its peak, even better. You'll see it appear to rise, pause, and reverse directions again as the earth turns. Because of the way the earth is tilted at the solstice, the sun sets farther from due west, with a shallower angle, and physically takes longer to set. Enjoy those long, romantic summer sunsets!

This is a great day for a backyard barbecue. Celebrate with fresh fruits of labor, whether they're vegetables and herbs from your garden or from a local farmers market. Decorate the table with wildflowers or sunflowers if you have them! The full moon in June is called the Strawberry Moon, and in Sweden, they celebrate the day by eating the first strawberries of the season.

If you live in an area that can have a bonfire, it would certainly be appropriate at this time of year as well. Take a hike and gather wildflowers or fresh herbs. Use a magnifying glass to examine local plants and flowers. Think about starting a compost bin for any plant scraps. My kids have fun going "camping" in the backyard. They gather all their equipment, including flashlights and snacks, and spend the evening chasing fireflies.

There are many outdoor activities you can do. Try making a pinwheel to catch the breeze, or get a hula hoop and see who can keep it spinning the longest. My daughter likes to decorate paper and fold it into a fan for hot afternoons. Make a faerie garden with upcycled items around the house, acorns, and rocks.

You can also try making a mason-bee house. Pack bamboo tubes tightly in a box or just tie them together with wire. Place them in an area near flowers or moist soil. They pack fertilized eggs, nectar, pollen, and finally, mud to plug the tub. This is done over and over to fill them. The larva feeds on the nectar and pollen loaf stored inside and forms a cocoon, hibernating over winter before emerging the following spring. You can move the house to a sheltered location if it's getting beaten up by winter winds and snow, but make sure to keep it outside or in a shed or an area with natural outdoor temperatures. Otherwise, the bees will hatch prematurely in the warmth of a shed or garage.

If you aren't feeling crafty, you can buy a bee house at a hardware store or visit a local honey farm. Local honey is soothing, antibacterial, an antioxidant, great for allergies, and full of natural prebiotics.

Goals

We are midway through the year. Well done! It's good to take a break and look back at the fruition of the projects you began in spring.

Take the time to celebrate your accomplishments. Align your celebratory actions with your completed goals. If you refinished your back patio, take an afternoon to enjoy it. Make a list of the things you accomplished or place check marks on your goal sheet. Bonus points if you use colorful pencils or stickers. Anything to make it special. You've earned it!

Think about your intentional goals. Have your relationships improved? Perfection is unattainable; celebrate progress and the path you've taken. Change can be difficult, but it doesn't come by shaming yourself into it. Love yourself enough to make healthy changes. You are an organic, living thing. What makes us different also makes us beautiful.

Rededicate yourself to your goals. You've laid the groundwork for this year's accomplishments and have more to come. Summer is a good milestone to pause and regather your energy.

Check in with your goals to make sure you're on track.

1. *Big-Picture Dream:* As with each season, I read back over my dream for inspiration. Find a sunny spot to open your notebook and envision your dream. You're chipping away at the steps to get there. Enjoy the feeling of it. Feel free to add details or artwork as your dream becomes alive.

2. *Annual Goals:* Review if you want to add, remove, or change anything.

3. *Affirmations:* Check in with your affirmations. Are they working for you? If not, consider changing them or

splitting them up into smaller chunks and rotating through 3-4 of them daily. I keep mine in my daily bullet journal or my activity planner so I can read a few each day. I can spend more intentional time thinking about them when there are just a few.

4. *Intentional-Goal Plans:* Review your goals. Make sure you're working towards your goals, and keep these changes alive and in your mind. Feel free to update or add notes as needed.

It takes a bit of time to read through these, so split them up over the next few weeks if needed. Change takes time, but you can do it! Anything is possible.

5. *Actionable-Goal Plans:* Read back through your plans. Update your calendar with the next two months' activities. Ensure you don't have any conflicts. Get into the right headspace for what you're planning on doing in the coming weeks.

At this midway point, check in to see how you're tracking on your overall plans. Adjust your goals or get advice and assistance wherever needed. Don't judge. Just review and decide the best course of action.

In Summary

As the momentum of the year reaches its high midpoint, reflect on the many accomplishments and lessons learned during the first half. Celebrate successes and enjoy the first fruits of your labor. Milestones are important, as they are significant stepping-stones to your goals. High momentum is unattainable in perpetuity. It's equally important to recognize this work. Enjoy the life and relationships you have built.

Use your achievements to drive your efforts and reaffirm your goals for the remainder of the year. You're halfway there already and have made great strides in the right direction. The seeds (metaphorically and figuratively) have been planted. It's time to water them, celebrate, pause, and prepare for the harvest to come.

Notice the abundance of life around you. Enjoy time outside, noticing the lush greenery and feeling the warm sun on your skin. You'll remember these moments in the dark cold of winter. Light signifies growth and expansion in this time of healing, empowerment, and movement. It is a time for growth and a time for joy.

Soak up the sun!

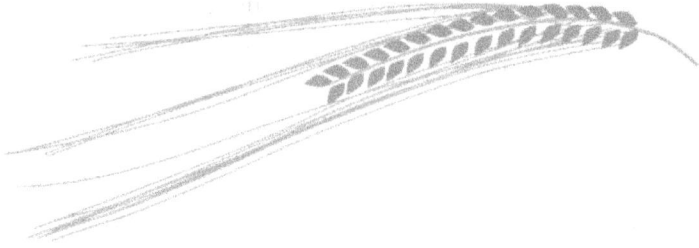

Midsummer

Overview
August 1 (Lammas Day)

Today marks the beginning of the harvest season. Historically, people would begin their harvest of cereal grains, wheat, oats, and barley. The first sheaves of wheat were ceremoniously harvested, ground, and made into a loaf of bread—the first of the new harvest. This loaf was blessed and broken in thankfulness for the harvest. Hlaf-maesse, or loaf-mass, changed to Lammas day in celebration.

Animals were brought in from the summer pasture, and milk was turned into cheese curd for the children, for luck and goodwill. The first barley stalks were turned into the first beer of the season. It was a major harvest festival, the first of the year.

Depending on the year, wheat may have run low prior to the harvest. Regardless of what stores may have looked like, the harvest was always celebrated as a reaping of what was sown throughout the season. All the planting and cultivating is done. All that's left is reaping the benefits. This is the same for us. All the hard work we've done throughout the year comes to fruition, and we can start to enjoy the fruits of our labor.

There's certainly summertime left, but after the peak of the summer solstice, the days are getting a little shorter each day and we can feel the slow shift into fall, even six weeks off.

This cycle has played out in many stories over the years. Greek mythology has Adonis, the grain god, so popular that he had the love of two women, Persephone and Aphrodite. Zeus, getting tired of the fighting over Adonis, ordered him to spend six months of the year with Persephone in the underworld and six months with Aphrodite. This was the Greeks' way of connecting with the vegetation producing half of the year and being dormant the other half.

Corn dollies were also made with corn husks from the harvest. They were kept indoors, near the hearth, in a prominent spot to honor the harvest and remind them of the cycle. The dolls were returned to the earth in the spring, adding to the plant matter that fertilized the soil. Seeds from the previous year's harvest were saved for the planting season the following year, passing symbolically and literally from harvest to harvest.

What to Do
Note the changing season outside. At the farmers market, the summer veggies are dying out, but corn is now readily available. The apples are beginning to ripen, but only the first summer apples are available. Summer festivals are in full swing, celebrating the harvests popular in those regions. Look online for local festivals and fairs in your area.

Today, it's easy to get bread and vegetables. We don't often think about how much work our previous generations had to do for their food, but that work made it easy for them to connect with the annual cycles of the earth.

We can drive to the grocery store and buy what we need, with very little fear that we will run out of the basics. Only a few generations ago, peoples' lives were at stake if they didn't get the harvest reaped at the right time or stored properly. People closely consulted the almanac and made notes for future years on the best timing and processes. Take the time to give thanks for what we have so readily available and the earth that provides so much for us.

This is also the time of year to honor the craftspersons and artisans. You can find them at the farmers markets, craft fairs, and renaissance fairs abundant this time of year. They worked during the early part of the year and, now, are out traveling, selling their wares. Do what you can to support them. Maybe even learn a new skill from them or try a craft at home.

Forget work for a day. Take a day in celebration of your efforts this year. Have a barbecue outside and enjoy the rest of the summer festivities. Set out a pool or sprinkler for the kids to play in; maybe even have fun with squirt guns or water balloons as a special treat to beat the remaining summer heat.

Try your hand at making bread, honoring our ancestors. I like to add any seeds and grains I have on hand to mix in my bread. Oat flour makes a nice consistency, as do a few tablespoons of oatmeal, flaxseed, barley, millet, or oat bran. Grains are typically very absorbent. Substitute about a tablespoon of flour for each tablespoon you add. If you're familiar with bread making, you'll be able to tell if it is too sticky and needs a bit more flour at the end.

Enjoy the last of the summer vegetables either from your garden or from the farmers markets. Make jams from the leftovers of the summer fruits. Reflect on what the rest of the year holds and how you might prepare for it. My mom always cans her extra tomatoes, cooked down with onion and bell peppers. Any one of these activities can mark the year and create a fun tradition tied to midsummer.

Goals

We're ready to reap some of the fruits of our labors! Take a note from our ancestors, and revel in the work accomplished this year. You still have work left in the year, but it's different work, wrapping up the year.

Look over your notes or journal, marking what you've completed so far. Life adds fun twists and turns. Some things might not have gone as planned. Others went better. We learn from each scenario. Take a moment to write down what you learned from each with no judgment.

Add things you did that were unplanned. Big or small, they are accomplishments. Take time to celebrate and feel it deeply.

1. *Big-Picture Dream:* As with each season, read back over your dream for inspiration. Find a sunny spot to envision your dream. You're chipping away at the steps to get there. Enjoy the feeling of it. Take your notes in celebration of what you achieved so far this year to encourage your thoughts and dreams. What have you enjoyed the most? What do you want your life to look like?

2. *Annual Goals:* Quickly review if you want to add, remove, or change anything. Think about the approaching end of the year and what you need to focus on. Prioritize.

3. *Affirmations:* Check in with your affirmations. Are you bullet-journaling them? Do you have them taped to your bathroom mirror? How ever it works for you, spend intentional time thinking about them.

4. *Intentional-Goal Plans:* Review your goals. Make sure you're working towards them, keeping these changes

alive and in your mind. Feel free to update or add notes as needed.

Take your time to read through these. Pick a few a day, or read through them at the beginning of the week. Find something that works for you to keep you in the right frame of mind.

5. *Actionable-Goal Plans:* Read back through your plans. It's time to update your calendar again! Look at the next two months of activities. Check for conflicts. Get ready for what you're planning on working on in the coming weeks.

In Summary

The harvest is gathered to supply food for the following year, and with it, seeds for the next year's rebirth, regeneration, and harvest. Your personal progress mirrors this. You've been working all year towards your goals and are setting positive habits that will be seeds for future years' planting and harvest.

Timing is important. Make notes for the future. Even today, you are transforming, creating new patterns to achieve the things that really matter to you. Think about your inner transformations, rebirth, and new beginnings.

As always, we take a designated celebration day for our accomplishments. Work is forgotten, and we rest, enriching ourselves in celebration. Summer is winding down. Enjoy some summer activities while we're in the season.

How to Fall!

Overview
September 21-23 (Fall Equinox)

Today marks the beginning of fall and the second harvest festival. It's time to harvest fruit trees, grapes, berries, corn, root vegetables, and squash. Most local wineries have festivals marking this time of year, complete with wine stomps and celebrations. Wineries often produce a Nouveau wine, made from the first harvest, with a short fermentation and fruity taste, to be enjoyed within the first year of bottling.

The fall equinox occurs when the sun crosses the equator from north to south, and like the spring equinox, the amount of day and night is equal. However, at this time of year, the days are shifting into darkness, with longer nights ahead. This shift is a sign that nature is winding down, reaching the final stage of its annual cycle of birth and death.

The trees and perennials reverse their energies, focusing them on their roots and away from the leaves, changing the colors into the beautiful fall ones we are so familiar with. The crops are becoming brown and dormant for the coming winter. The bounty of crops from the orchard is carefully packed into storage with the grains from the fields.

Historically, this would be a time for thanksgiving for the year's harvest, enjoying the last of the perishable foods, and appreciating the abundance reaped.

Depending on where you live, you may be seeing varying levels of fall. Currently, we're having a longer-than-normal summer, but even though the weather is still warm, I can see definitive signs of the coming season. Leaves are slowly changing and falling off the trees. Plants are dying and drying out. There's a different feeling in the air that reminds me of fall, even with the still-warm temperatures.

Apples are a symbol of wisdom and guidance. As the tree slowly wanes, the seeds within the apple represent the rebirth of life in the coming year.

What to Do
See what changes are happening in your area. Are the leaves changing color or falling to cover the ground around them? If you live near any local farms, you'll notice the fields are becoming bare. Corn will dry out in the fields and be harvested. Field mice start looking for somewhere to hide from the coming cold. Farmers markets are closing for the season.

Instead of being depressed about the coming darkness, I tend to look forward to the time of year when I can slow down and wrap myself up in cozy things. The changing weather brings out boots and scarves, fall colors, hot cocoa, and the ever-beloved pumpkin-spiced latte. Whether or not you love PSL, you probably have a favorite fall food or tradition.

Try going to a local high-school football game even if you don't have any kids in the school. Make sure you bring a nice warm blanket and some hot chocolate. Our local high school has a fun Homecoming Parade each fall. I look forward to seeing the vendors and grabbing a coffee and a pork-chop sandwich to watch the parade. It's generally a chilly day, and I grab a hat and scarf to keep me warm in the crisp air as I listen to the sound of the band and watch the fire trucks go by.

If you have a local winery, try going to their harvest festival. Our local winery has a grape stomp, complete with an *I Love Lucy* costume contest. We buy a bottle of Nouveau wine to enjoy on the equinox on a blanket outdoors.

Look for a holistic retreat in the area, something outdoors, like outdoor yoga, focused on rejuvenation and healing. Local apple orchards often have festivals with apple picking, hay bales, and apple baked goods to enjoy. We like to pick a bag of apples and feed the goats at our local orchard's petting zoo. It's a fun afternoon that the kids look forward to each year. Don't forget to bring some apple butter, apple cider, or apple-cider doughnuts home!

As with the harvest season, enjoy the ripe, freshly picked apples. I love making an apple crisp; it feels uniquely fall to me, full of cinnamon and cardamom. Try roasting some root vegetables. Roast a sheet pan of mixed roots, like beets, turnips, potatoes, carrots, parsnips, and rutabaga. Toss them in a little olive oil, sea salt, and pepper. Add the turnips to the pan ten minutes after you add the rest, as they don't take as long to cook. Veggies get a wonderful, sweet flavor when roasted.

I don't grow enough tomatoes in my garden to can, but I do have quite a bit when the plants are producing well. Typically, I store the surplus of ripe tomatoes in a big stock pot in the fridge until I have enough to make a large batch of marinara. I use fresh basil, oregano, and garlic from my garden, with a little red wine for flavor. The family always looks forward to spaghetti and lasagna with marinara from our gardens' tomatoes. I cook it down a bit more for a homemade pizza sauce. If I have enough, they can be frozen for future use.

I like drying herbs for winter. I don't grow all my own vegetables or herbs, but the act of growing a few things and storing them connects me in a small way to the cycles of the land. I enjoy taking time of the weekend to clip some basil, oregano, lavender, chives, sage, and chamomile. Some, I hang to dry in my garage. The rest are cleaned and laid out on cookie sheets in my garage to dry for a week or two before crumbling them to store in clean jars. Sometimes, I make batches of pesto to freeze for winter use.

If you're not a fan of dried herbs, try making a paste with fresh herbs and olive oil in your food processor. You can freeze it in ice-cube trays. The oil insulates the herbs from oxygen. Pop a cube into simmering marinara for a fresh-tasting reminder of summer.

Decorate your house with fall items. I love the bowl of apples sitting on my kitchen table. Bring in acorns and colorful leaves you come across on walks. You can even make a basket or cornucopia with fruits and berries for the table. Tie some red, gold, orange, and yellow ribbons to decorate. Add warm candles throughout the house.

Our ancestors would have taken time to celebrate the harvest, then carefully store it for winter. During this time, they would have also cleared out unnecessary items to make room for the harvest and shared the surplus with those less fortunate.

As you look to find balance in your life, consider donating items you no longer need. Preparing for winter, I find it easier to purge unneeded things. I believe there's a reason that we have donations for food pantries and other goodwill organizations this time of year. It feels good to give back and clean out what you don't need. Consider donating some of your time to community outreach programs, which are typically abundant this time of year.

Gather with friends and family for a little thanksgiving of your own, whether at a dinner party, a garden party, or an outdoor bonfire with s'mores. Practice gratitude with harvest cards you can share. Whatever you do, I hope you find some fun new traditions to enjoy this beautiful holiday and share it with those around you.

Goals

We are nearing the end of our annual goals. We have made another large push towards getting things done and choosing priorities for the remainder of the year. Just as animals prepare for hibernation, as we wrap up our work, remember that we are stocking up for the winter months. In goal terms, we are making a little headway on projects in preparation for moving indoors during the winter.

Before we make that final push, as always, we need to celebrate our successes over the past six weeks. Check in on your goals. Focus on what you did complete. Make sure to take time for the things that matter most. You are trying to realize your goals, but you can't sacrifice the life you have already built. Balance these two carefully, as they are *both* important.

1. *Big-Picture Dream:* Again, read back over your dream for inspiration. Find an outside spot to reflect and envision your dream. You're moving closer each day. Can you see it? Make notes of what you accomplished and what you feel thankful for. Allow this to inspire you.

2. *Annual Goals:* Review if you want to add, remove, or change anything. We are nearing the end of the year. Think about what you need to wrap up. Move things around as needed. Prioritize.

3. *Affirmations:* Check in with your affirmations. Have you been doing them daily, weekly, or at least occasionally? Have they helped? What could you do differently to

make them more effective? There is no right or wrong answer. The goal is to keep them in mind. If they're difficult, shorten them, do them less often, or not at all. It's your process and your progress. Make it work for you.

4. *Intentional-Goal Plans:* Review your goals. Keep them alive. As always, feel free to update or add notes as needed. Take your time. It doesn't have to be done all in one day. Have faith in yourself.

You are capable of far more than you imagine.

5. *Actionable-Goal Plans:* Read back through your plans. It's that time to update your calendar again! This time, look over the next three months. You're almost at the end of the year, with the final push coming soon. Prioritize. Check for conflicts. Be kind to yourself about what you can accomplish. Adjust your annual goals if needed.

Personal lives and plans change. Acknowledge the fact that you can't always do everything. You may have been a bit overzealous in planning for the year. It's very possible that you need to remove things from your list this year. If so, start a short list for the following year. Don't go into detail. You'll have time during winter to do this. Just make a list of items you need to eliminate and set aside. This is not failure. It's growth to recognize and learn your limits.

In Summary
Proper preparation in fall has always been massively important for human survival. Even though your livelihood is not likely at risk, focus on stocking up and completing tasks to prepare for a healing and celebratory winter. You want to take more time for yourself than normal, so plan for it.

Be mindful of the changes in temperature and clothes, from cold drinks to warm ones. Reflect on the changes outside and inside.

As we move closer to the colder months, home and family will take center stage. Move priorities and activities around to accomplish only what's required. Embrace change, but prepare in a positive way and take clues from the world around you for these moments that cause disruption and growth.

Mid-Fall

Overview
October 31 (Halloween/Samhain)

Most widely recognized as Halloween, the celebration of this day is twofold. It's not only a time for play, dressing up, going door-to-door for candy, and saying, "Trick or Treat!" It is also a day of remembrance.

In Catholicism, this holiday is a triduum, or a 3-day religious holiday, called Allhallowtide. It starts with All Hallows' Eve (Oct 31st), commonly known as Halloween, absorbing some of the Celtic Samhain traditions of honoring those who have passed. The Celts believed the veil between the living and the afterlife was thinnest at this time. They would honor their ancestors and attempt to communicate with them. Some dressed up, thinking it would protect them from anything malevolent. The church would hold an all-night vigil and fast in preparation for the feast to come.

All Saints' Day, All Hallows, or Hallowmas (Nov 1st) was reserved for remembrance of the saints, known and unknown. A feast is held to honor them. All Souls' Day, the final day of Allhallowtide (Nov 2nd), is used to remember all other souls.

Many observers visit graveyards and place flowers on gravestones.

In Mexico, people celebrate Día de Muertos, or the Day of the Dead, from Oct 31st to Nov 2nd. It's a time to commemorate the lives of those who have passed, particularly the ancestors. It's more of a celebration than a somber day. They may serve the honored departed's favorite foods, set out photos, light candles, dress as the deceased, or visit graves with gifts.

Some cultures have a Dumb Supper, where you set a single place at the table for all those who have passed. The plate is served like everyone else's, sometimes with the deceased's favorite foods. The entire meal is silent, meant to be spent in solemn reflection of the honored souls that have passed. The plate is then taken outside and left overnight for nature.

The carving of the pumpkin originated from carving turnips and potatoes, and lighting them to scare away harmful spirits. It marked the third and final harvest season of the year in North America. Digging up root vegetables and gathering nuts and berries was done at this time. It was important to store all the available food for winter, and this was the final chance to pack the cellars.

Today, we carve or paint pumpkins, decorate with spooky or fun themes, and dress up for candy. Mums are added to the porch or planted in the garden, and pumpkin spice is added to practically everything from candy to baked goods or drinks.

What to Do
It's easy to see the changes this time of year. Depending on where you live, the leaves change color and drop off. This time of the year is associated with death, and we can literally see it all around us. But instead of thinking of death as a negative or scary thing, try to connect it with the cycle of life and rebirth that we will experience in the spring.

Think back over the year, and remember what you have lost. This doesn't mean only people or items. It could be a job or a bad habit. Positive or negative, reflect on it and let it go. Write something you're trying to let go of on a piece of paper, and burn it in a bonfire or fireplace.

Bonfires are common in the fall. Have friends over and prepare a deep, rich stew filled with root vegetables. Make caramel corn or candied pecans. Even though the farmers markets are largely closed by now, root vegetables and squash are still readily available. Bags of nuts and dried berries are easy to find as well. Set out a bowl of nuts or add dried berries to cookies and cakes.

One of my friends even turned his holiday (painted) pumpkin into pumpkin bars and brought them for one of our bonfire nights. What a fun way to reuse his pumpkin! Add cinnamon, nutmeg, allspice, ginger, or cardamom to foods like stews and baked goods. Another of my friends brought a spiced ginger-pear cocktail with bits of diced pear. It would be easy to make this into a punch for kids.

One of the more interesting things I do is make a fruitcake. I know it has a long history of being an unappetizing brick of a cake, passed around, unwanted, from friend to friend. However, good fruitcakes are filled with dried or candied fruits and nuts, then basted in marmalade and brandy or rum for six weeks. I'm personally more of a fruit-pie person, but I do like the spices and flavor. My husband and mom, however, love it. The cake is a labor of love, and I enjoy all the steps and time it takes to make it, even though it's a lot of work.

I chop the dried and candied fruits, adding in a cup of rum and a cup of mulled apple cider, left over from bonfire night. Brown sugar, the zest and juice of one lemon, and one orange go in, as well as tons of spices. Everything is simmered together for 10 min, and then sits overnight. By the next day, the fruits have expanded and absorbed the spiced liquids, leaving a very thick syrup and plumped-up fruits. I add toasted pecans, walnuts, and a mixture of different flours, baking it for an hour. Then I baste the hot cake with orange marmalade and a little brandy. After cooling, it's turned out on a clean linen cloth to be basted with rum.

Every 3-7 days, I unfold the cloth and brush on more rum, patting and smelling the fruitcake baby. I can't explain why I love to make it so much. I think it's because of the lengthy process. I love all the steps: toasting the nuts to add flavor, taking time to add love and care. It's beautiful and smells great. When it's unwrapped at Christmas, my family extols its virtue, talking around full bites of cake and whipped cream. I love to know that I took the time all season long to make this for them. It's Christmastime, and isn't that the name of the game, taking the time to show your family how much they mean to you?

While we have never held a Dumb Supper, we do have a candle service before dinner. We bring out pictures or funeral cards of those we want to remember. Tealights are scattered on the table, lit one by one with the reading of each name and placing the item on the table with a moment to retrospect. Sometimes, we say a few words about them, who they were, or what they meant to us. We have collars and tags to honor beloved pets that have passed. It's a moving ceremony, and tears often make an appearance, but so does love. If we allow ourselves to talk about our loved ones who have passed, we honor the value they have in our lives. Don't be ashamed of getting emotional; it only nods at the value held in our hearts.

Among all the holiday planning, remember to prepare for winter. Sometimes, this means making Christmas lists or menus for Thanksgiving and Christmas/Yule. It's also a good time to put away your water hoses if you live in a place that freezes. I put away my hummingbird feeders and turn off any water sources that could freeze. Sweep off the porches, and put away any lawn furniture that could get ruined by snow. I move my snow shovels from my shed to my garage and get out the hats, gloves, and snow boots in preparation.

I love all seasons, but I *really* love this time of year, when the world winds down and the holidays are approaching. The smell of dried leaves and the sound of them crunching underfoot are nostalgic. Falling leaves are among the most beautiful things I've ever seen in nature. I take great pleasure in seeing them swirl on the road or pepper a pathway. Standing outside and watching the colorful leaves actively drop, making their slow descent to the grass, littered with more color, fills me with awe. Take time to go visit a coffee shop with friends or family. Sit at peace over a warm cup of frothy coffee or cocoa.

Goals

This is it! Our final wrap-up in preparation for winter. While our livelihood isn't dependent on our preparations in this modern age, there are several responsibilities we have within our own lives that need to be tended to. Whether at home, at work, or toward our personal goals.

Look back over your goals for the year, and make a new list this time. At the top of it, write "Accomplishments." Ensure that you write down each and every thing you made time for or to further yourself, even the things that came up unexpectedly that you had to take care of. This list can be as exhaustive or as high-level as you wish. Make sure to add personal-growth items, such as obstacles you had to overcome or skills you had to learn. I often have trouble asking others for help. Being brave enough to reach out is an obstacle I often have to overcome.

Take your celebration time a little quieter this year, in a bit of reflection on these accomplishments. As you look back over what you have left to wrap up the year, keep your successes in mind.

1. *Big-Picture Dream:* Remember, this is why you're doing the work. You've already made steps toward attaining your dreams. Your list of accomplishments shows the hard work you've done. Think of how the steps you've made and your priorities this year propel you toward your dream.

   If your steps aren't moving you toward your dream, take a moment to reflect on that. Not to judge it, but to think about why. It may be that you have a different dream and need to make changes. Or it may be that you are letting other things come between you and your priorities. Acknowledge it and adjust.

2. *Annual Goals:* Look over your remaining goals. You should be near the end of the list.

3. *Affirmations:* Think about your affirmations. Are they working for your goals? Jot some thoughts down about this. Next year, you can use this knowledge to improve them further. Practice what's important to you.

4. *Intentional-Goal Plans:* Review your goals and thank yourself for your work this year. Are you in a better place than you were at the beginning of the year? Where have you seen the most progress? Why?

5. *Actionable-Goal Plans:* You only have six weeks left. Check your list and your calendar. Fit in what you can, but only what you must. If you need to move things to next year's list, do so without negative emotions.

In Summary

Take time to celebrate the year. Think about what you've gained, and give thanks for it. Think about what you've lost, and release it. Think about what you've learned from it, and appreciate it.

Celebrate the memory of those who have passed: our ancestors who paved the way for us, setting up life so we may prosper, and our loved ones that we have lost. Celebrate the memory of yourself at different stages in your life. Reflect on your many accomplishments this year, giving thanks for every one of them.

Focus on any final things to wrap up the year in preparation for winter. Enjoy the process, and pay attention to your growth.

In Conclusion

December 20-23 (Winter Solstice / Christmas / Yule)

You've made it! You achieved everything you set out to do. If you didn't complete everything from your initial plan last winter, you still completed the years' work. Whatever you succeeded in is enough.

You may have had to adjust your expectations, but if you followed along, you at least achieved that. In our modern life, it's rare that people complete anything. You made progress! Appreciate yourself for completing this activity and whatever adjusted plan you finished.

Pull out your accomplishments list, and update it for the remainder of the year. It's now completed! Take a solitary moment with a glass of warm cider, tea, or wine. Sit with the list, and reflect on what you were able to do when you set your mind to it while connecting with the cycle of the earth.

The earth gives us seasons; don't take them for granted. All seasons have beauty, even winter, and many gifts can be found throughout the year. Look for them. Notice them. Cherish them.

As you enjoy the holiday season, go back to the beginning of the book and start over in your yearly cycle of goal plans and healing renewal. Your future year plans may look different, now that you've done a full year. They may be more detailed or much simpler. Make them your own.

This is a time to stay in, take care of yourself and reflect. Spend time with your family and enjoy the slow, darker time. Continue to follow the book each season, growing and changing as needed. Remember to push forward firmly, but not too hard. To realize your dreams, learn from every step.

Your big-picture dream should always be kept special and pure. Don't ever forget to *dream big* and *dream free*. When you work towards each year's goal, remember your dreams first. Then see what could be accomplished that year to get you to your goal. Only then is logic allowed back into the playing field. It's appropriate because this is logic's job, to plan and detail what's accomplishable at that moment.

I wouldn't recommend adjusting your dream because of what's logically accomplishable. Often, the best ideas come when we remove restrictions from our mind. You don't want to build them into your dream. We can actually stop our goals from happening if we believe we can't attain them. We turn away from opportunities because of fear. Changes will come; however, as you live your best life and your dream comes into fruition, piece by piece, with calmness and loving acceptance. It's there you'll find a lovely balance of the two, one in which you have full control. You are far greater than you ever dreamed to be.

Historically, special events are made more meaningful with rituals and ceremonies, just like a marriage ceremony makes reverent the bond of two people. Traditions are a way to memorialize and commemorate the community and family, strengthen ties, and mark the passage of time. If you've ever had little children in the household, you know their excitement adds so much magic to the holidays as they look forward to the traditions they've made in the past. Every time you redo one of these traditions, such as baking cinnamon rolls for Christmas Eve or making Christmas cookies as a family, you strengthen that memory and the time-marking bond it has.

By adding some celebrations and traditions into our lives, we not only enjoy more community with our family and friends, but we connect with nature a bit more. We bond with it, noticing things we didn't before, feeling a connection with the earth that supports and provides for us. We literally couldn't live without the symbiotic relationship with nature's oxygen-creating plants.

Add meaning to your life while honoring the passage of time, and practice the art of living seasonally.

From the Author:
I hope you enjoyed this book. It was a passion project of mine, a little thank you, honoring the world around us and the beauty in everyday life.

I sincerely hope you have gained something from this, noticed a small thing in nature, or made some steps towards your own dream. This book is part of my personal dream. It makes my heart happy that you were a part of it!

Author Bio:
Willa Daniels is a fictional character created by author Jen Flanagan, a certified herbalist living in the Pacific Northwest. If you're interested in hearing more about Willa's adventures with her friends, her newfound magical abilities, and finding love, check out *Saltwater Cures (Orca Cove Series Book One)*.

If you enjoyed this book, the nicest thing you can do is leave me a good review on Amazon, Goodreads, Bookbub, or anywhere you review books.

Connect with me online:
Website: **jenflanaganbooks.com**
Follow Willa on Amazon
Facebook: **@jenflanaganbooks**
Instagram: **@jenflanagan_author**
Bookbub: **@willa_daniels**

Please visit my blog at **jenflanaganbooks.com** for upcoming books, comments, and minor musings.

What's Next?

I've got several more non-fiction books in the works as part of The Natural Path series. The first, *An Introduction to Herbalism,* is out now. *An Introduction to Soap Making*, *Home and Cleaning Solutions*, and *Body and Skincare Solutions* will be coming in 2024.

Stay tuned, friends!

Jen Flanagan Fiction Books

Orca Cove Series:
Saltwater Cures
Uncharted Waters (coming 2024)

Books in the Detective Malone Series:
Bad Company
Here I Go Again
Under Pressure

Willa Daniels Non-Fiction Books

Stand-alone books:
The Art of Living Seasonally

The Natural Path Series:
An Introduction to Herbalism
An Introduction to Soap Making (coming 2024)
Home and Cleaning Solutions (coming 2024)
Body and Skincare Solutions (coming 2024)